The Five-Minute Druid

Connection Made Easy

The Five-Minute Druid

Connection Made Easy

Sarah-Beth Watkins

**MOON
BOOKS**

Winchester, UK
Washington, USA

JOHN HUNT PUBLISHING

First published by Moon Books, 2024
Moon Books is an imprint of John Hunt Publishing Ltd., No. 3 East Street, Alresford
Hampshire SO24 9EE, UK
office@jhpbooks.net
www.johnhuntpublishing.com
www.moon-books.net

For distributor details and how to order please visit the 'Ordering' section on our website.

Text copyright: Sarah-Beth Watkins 2023

ISBN: 978 1 80341 380 8
978 1 80341 381 5 (ebook)
Library of Congress Control Number: 2022948096

A CIP catalogue record for this book is available from the British Library.

Design: Lapiz Digital Services

UK: Printed and bound by CPI Group (UK) Ltd, Croydon, CR0 4YY
Printed in North America by CPI GPS partners

We operate a distinctive and ethical publishing philosophy in
all areas of our business, from our global network of authors to
production and worldwide distribution.

Contents

Introduction

Bah, I hear you say! Druids died out years ago! But you picked up this book so somewhere inside, somewhere deep, you are interested in Druidry. You want to know more and you'd love to be one but you're not sure how to go about it and surely Druidry really isn't relevant today. Or perhaps you've dabbled before, started a course, read a few books and then stalled. Or you are returning to your path and just need some tips to move you forward.

Yes, the old druids died out. The ones who supposedly wore white robes with sickles and mistletoe in their belts, the ones who made their last stand at Anglesey against the Roman invaders, and the ones who revived druidic practices in the nineteenth century – of course, they died out but they left behind a legacy – ways of looking at the world, ways of communing with nature, old stories, myths and legends and today's modern druids take that all on board and create their own practice with the knowledge left by these druids and with the wisdom of today. Some belong to groups or groves, others are solitary or hedge druids. But each and every one honours nature.

So what exactly is Druidry?

Druidry is a spiritual practice based on the love of nature and all it encompasses – the earth, sea, sky, trees, plants, animals – and us. The us that has disconnected from the old ways, the us whose ancestors honoured the land with celebration, the us who now faces ecological disaster – and Druidry is never more important than it is today in the face of what we, in modern times, have done to our earth.

Druidry involves getting out and about (if you can) and connecting on a deeper level with your surroundings, the environment, the wheel of the year, the elements, honouring the land, connecting with trees, plants and animals and much more – in fact its quite a mixture and every druid develops their own version of their practice and their own path. Some practices come easy, others not so much but overtime everyone works out the best way for themselves to honour the elements of Druidry in their life.

What Druidry is not is a dogmatic religion. There are no rules here. There is no bible, no set way to honour deities – you don't have to honour them at all, let alone worship them – and no prayers unless you want to say them – instead it is a collection of ideas and practices that you can dip in and out of to find your own way. Nothing is set in stone and there is no one right way to be a druid. There are organisations to become a part of that can give you more structure if you like but you can also be a hedge druid working it out for yourself on your own as you go along.

But what if we can't work it out? What if we are struggling to include Druidry in our daily lives but really want to do more, to find out more? You could be flat out at work with not a minute to spare, have a new baby in the house and many sleepless nights, or you could be housebound or recovering from an illness. Whatever the reasons, life sometimes throws up challenges that get in the way of practicing Druidry as much as we would like. We can't get out, we don't have much time, we feel disconnected and it's so difficult to consider our nature spirituality in amongst the daily grind. Or something happens that brings us to a halt.

I'm relatively new to what I would call my organised druidic practice but throughout my life, I have always followed the path in various ways. I'm a nature lover, animal lover, tree hugger – call me what you will – but I never called myself a druid. I've dabbled in divination, welcomed the sun in the morning and honoured my ancestors but it all came naturally and without any focus. Then I went on holiday to a magical place, an historic old house with a rath (hill fort) in the garden that had been turned into a walled sanctuary and I sat there on the grass and in the sun with my dog to do some research on a book I was writing. Among the books I'd taken with me was some light reading (!) *The Book of English Magic* by Philip Carr-Gomm and Richard Heygate, a look at the history of magical lore and practice in England containing everything from witches and alchemists to freemasons and adepts of the Rosy Cross in it. And as I read the chapter on druids – well – it just spoke to me. Whatever notions I had of mistletoed men in white robes dancing amongst the trees vanished. Druids were real and I was one of them!

After that I probably ordered every book on Amazon about Druidry, absorbed everything like a sponge and then this year I decided to really concentrate on my path. But then I had an accident that put me out of action for two months. For the first couple of weeks, I moved between the bed and the bathroom and that was it! I was stopped in my tracks at a time when my spiritual beliefs were most needed.

As I lay there in my misery – yes absolutely wallowing in it – and regretting that I couldn't get out I began to wonder what I could do. I knew if I started to do something – however small – it would make me feel better, support my healing and stop me from thinking solely about myself and my predicament. So I began with little bite-sized ways of continuing my practice and found small ways to start connecting again.

This book is packed with tips and suggestions for small five-minute ways to bring Druidry into your life. We'll look at key elements of nature spirituality including noticing and observing, daily practice, honouring the ancestors and deities, the wheel of the year, the elements and connecting with trees and also ways in which you can find inspiration and meaning through reading and listening, writing and drawing, social media and apps and quick and easy, five-minute creative projects.

Some of the ideas could take longer if you are able, while others can be as short as you want them to be but all of them can help you to include Druidry in your life – even for the briefest moment. This is a guide to connecting with nature in simple, practical ways, taking pleasure from the smallest things and finding your way again.

Chapter 1

Just Notice

One of the best ways to be with nature is, of course, to get outside. But not everyone has the time to take a long walk in the countryside, to ramble through a forest or kick sand along a beach. Not everyone is able to go for a walk full stop so that's why this chapter focuses on walking but more importantly, noticing.

For those of us who can get out for a walk – great – the tips that follow can help but if you've got time for a leisurely stroll then you probably aren't struggling with reconnecting. However, if you are dashing around from place to place – work, school, shops, wherever, in an ongoing, never-ending loop – then this is about stopping for five minutes. Just five in all that mayhem. It could be while you are waiting for a bus, standing in the queue to collect the kids or on the commute. Many of us don't stop to notice and observe the outside world during our daily routines. We are so busy moving from pillar to post and caught up in our own thoughts that we don't look at what is around us, not enough to really notice it.

If you are housebound or can't get out, this is about finding a window from which you can at least see some plants, trees, the sky, and even a bird table or feeder – a view of nature – however small it may be. You might think that your daily routine is boring or you are so sick of being indoors you're not going to see anything new from your window but nature will surprise you and in that surprise, in that heightened awareness of the world around you, you will regain connection.

By just taking five minutes a day or even as little as once a week, we can start to reconnect to the land, our surroundings and to our path. We can sense our place and our space allowing us to once more feel a part of the earth, nature and all its glories.

Whether you are out and about or looking from a window, consciously tell yourself you are taking your five minutes and breathe deeply for three long, slow breaths. In and out, in and out, in and out. If you can, close your eyes while you concentrate on your breathing and centre yourself.

Open your eyes and then notice – really notice – your view, however big or small it is.

Pick one thing to notice and focus on in that day's five minutes of observation which could include:

- What way are you facing? Orient yourself by noticing whether you are facing north, south, east or west. What element is associated with that direction? Think about what that element means to you.
- What season is it? The wheel of the year acknowledges the solstices and the equinoxes. Look to see what signs there are of that time of the year. Are there any signs of the next season to come?
- What trees can you see? Can you identify them all? How old do you think they are?
- What plants or flowers grow in your local environment? Take notice of even the smallest weeds. Even in the most built-up of places, nature will have found a way to survive.
- Is there any wildlife? Any birds? Do you know what they are? Do you know anything about them – what they eat, where they sleep, the tracks they leave?
- What can you hear? Is it all just background noise or if you can block that out, can you hear birds singing, the wind in the trees, or a distant trickle of water?
- What can you touch? If you are stuck inside, imagine what you could touch if you were outside your window.

- What is the weather doing? Relate it back to the wheel of the year – is it usual for that season?
- What does the sky look like? Are there clear indications of a sunny or stormy day ahead? Can you see anything in the clouds?
- Do you know what time the sun is currently setting and rising?

Pick one thing to focus on and the next time you have five minutes pick another. It may not be practical but you could time your five minutes to purposely see something that we take for granted every day. Build up a picture of what is happening in your local environment. If you can, try this at different times of the day and see what differences there are. Even if you are treading the same path or looking from the same old window, the wheel of the year keeps turning and there will be fresh, new things to notice.

For example, through one of my windows, I can see a bird table. Once the food is out, crows, wood pigeons and magpies descend but then the smaller birds come out. After the initial feeding frenzy there are different visitors throughout the day. The robins don't like to land on the table but feed under it and the blackbirds ignore it altogether and search for worms, especially after rain. By just having a focus, even seen through a window, you can learn so much more about your environment.

Another technique is to find a sit spot – a place where you go to whenever you can – to sit and just observe the world around you. By going to that same place, over and over, in different seasons, at different times, you will start to notice the changes around you. I have a flat stone hidden in a grass verge along an estuary. Its been there for years now and gives me a perch whether it's sunny or raining. And as far as I know, I'm the only one that uses it – although others are most welcome! From there

I can see across the fields and notice the colours of the land and how they change depending on the season. I can see the fields being cut for hay or the cows being put out to pasture. I can watch the tide go in and out, the birds that feed in the mud, the fish that jump up from the shallows and lots more. But I also know I am extremely lucky to have such a place close by that I can go to every day. Is there somewhere you can go to – even in an urban environment – where you can notice and observe the world around you? The same spot you eat lunch or the same spot you wait for the kids to come out of school? Can you pull a chair up to a window so you create your own inside sit spot? Finding a sit spot will help you to notice the changes around you but also give you a place to find peace, a place to still your mind and to just feel connected once again.

Noticing what you can in the day, however, is completely different to what is around you at night. For some of us, the night is a scary time and there is no better place than being cosy and secure indoors. I'm not advocating you compromise your safety and security by going out at night but if you can, try to observe the differences between night and day. Sit in your garden for five minutes, open that window or watch from the back door.

- What phase of the moon is apparent?
- Can you see any stars? Do you know their names or can pick out any constellations?
- Is there wildlife – foxes, bats, hedgehogs? You might like to attract some species by leaving out some food.
- Are there any birds still singing or calling?
- What about the insects that are drawn to the window or other light sources?

Build on your observations by noting what you see at different times of the year. Jotting it all down in a notebook or journal will probably take more than five minutes and if you've really been feeling disconnected then writing it all down can seem a chore. I use the note function on my phone – it literally takes a minute – to remind myself of things I want to look up later. Or take a picture of something you can't identify and look into that at another time (see Social Media and Apps chapter).

I'm lucky enough to live close to several beaches and I have walked my dog in the same spot too many times to count, as well as his predecessors before him, over and over again. Until I began doing this exercise I was in walk mode but not notice mode. I would stride along for an hour or more just trying to get the daily walk done so I could rush back to work but then I learnt to stop.

I have found species of plants I never realised grew there, nooks and crevices to explore that I didn't know existed before and animal tracks that I could have easily walked over. I've been lucky to see foxes eating fish on the banks of the estuary, hawks wheeling in the sky, and fish jumping from the water with water glistening from their scales – truly magnificent sights – but I have also taken great joy from noticing bee holes, sloes growing, spider webs coated with dew in the morning, new buds on the trees, caterpillars on the march and butterflies dancing in the sunshine. The small things are important, the details bring the natural world to life.

And what noticing does is it links you to nature and to your Druidry path. The more you notice, the more you are connecting. By stilling your mind and opening yourself up to the natural world, even for just five minutes, you are taking in so much. You are learning what is around you and how it all fits together, yourself included. Nature's wonders can be found in the smallest details – you just need to notice them.

Chapter 2

Daily Practice

There is a saying that if you ask five druids what Druidry means you will get ten different answers. This is nowhere more apparent than in what constitutes someone's daily practice. Some call them devotions but devotion is a loaded word and where some see a religious aspect to nature spirituality, others don't. Some like the comfort of a daily prayer or ritual, whilst others don't – some even argue about the terms 'ritual' and 'prayer'.

So this chapter is going to suggest ways in which you can honour your daily commitment to Druidry, your commitment to nature spirituality and your commitment to yourself as a part of it. Noticing as we looked at in Chapter 1 is one form of a daily practice and if that is all you can manage right now then that is fine but here are some other ideas to reaffirm your path on a daily basis in just five minutes.

A lot of literature will tell you to start your day the right way with a daily practice. It doesn't take much longer than a few minutes for instance to align yourself with the four quarters and give thanks and blessings to the north, east, south and west.

But if like me, you get woken up by a dog scratching at the door, a cat miaowing for its breakfast, or a child wanting something, then that first five minutes is gone. I find myself saying a quick good morning to the sun and then I'm off. Grab a cup of tea, start the chores, and head to work. But somewhere in there, you could snatch five minutes or less.

- If you have a slow, clunky kettle like mine, is there a minute there to give thanks for the water that you are boiling?

- As you spread butter and jam on your toast, could you give thanks for the fruits that were used to make that delicious spread?
- When you slam the front door, can you send a silent prayer up of thanks for your home and the people in it and head off with a blessing that all will be safe and well when you are gone?

Sometimes rather than making extra time for your practice it can be easier to incorporate it into what you already do. Of course, having peace and quiet to completely concentrate on your path is the ideal to aspire to but it doesn't necessarily work every day.

For days when you can spend that five minutes in solitude, find a morning devotional that speaks to you and that is easy to remember. The OBOD (Order of Bards, Ovates and Druids) prayer for instance, adapted from *Barddas* by Iolo Morganwg, is:

Grant, O Great Spirit/Goddess/God/Holy Ones, Thy Protection;
And in protection, strength;
And in strength, understanding;
And in understanding, knowledge;
And in knowledge, the knowledge of justice;
And in the knowledge of justice, the love of it;
And in that love, the love of all existences;
And in the love of all existences, the love of Great Spirit/
Goddess/God/Holy Ones/the Earth our mother, and all
goodness.

But there are all different versions and there are several websites that give suggestions such as www.prairiedruid.com and www. druidryus.org. The druid vow is also easy to remember and recite. Although normally used in groves and during ritual, it can be adapted to use as an individual whilst perhaps imagining you are in your sacred grove with other like-minded people:

I swear by peace and love to stand
Heart to heart, and hand in hand;
Mark! O Spirit, and hear me now,
Confirming this, my sacred vow.

There are also books like Caitlin Matthew's *Celtic Devotional*, AODA's *The Druid's Book of Ceremonies, Prayers and Songs* and *Druid Songs: Poetry of Prayer and Praise for the Druid Kind* by G.R. Grove that can give you simple and easy suggestions for your own practice and if you are struggling with devotionals and/or remembering them, you could also try writing your own.

Consider simple ways to start the day with a nod to your druidic path with an affirmation. Something as simple as a sentence like 'Today I will endeavour to walk the path of nature' or 'Today I will connect more with trees'. You can expand your affirmation to be as long as you like. For instance, think of your senses and what you hope to feel – 'Today I want to connect with nature, feel the wind in my hair, water on my face and the earth beneath my shoes'. And you can, of course, change it from day to day.

Many druids have an altar or sacred space (a term I prefer!) where they collect meaningful objects – things that speak to them of their path. Mine consists of plants, carved pieces of wood, goddess ornaments, fossils, crystals, feathers, and candles – some things I have purchased, some I have made but most of them I have found. When you are on your walk or doing your noticing, see if there is something that you can take home to put in your sacred space. It can be as small as a pebble, a leaf or a flower or as large as a piece of driftwood, a sprig of holly or an interesting rock. As you go about your daily routine, look out for things to add – a feather that has blown into your path, an odd-shaped stone, a wind-blown leaf from your favourite tree. You'll find that you'll soon come up with quite a collection!

You can regularly change your sacred space to give it focus or have more than one – there is no limit. You could have an outside space as well as inside spaces. It doesn't have to be big, impressive or filled with the most expensive ornaments. I have a statue in the garden that I leave small gifts next to – a pebble from the beach, a sheaf of wheat, or a sea-smoothed shard of pottery. I also put something extra in my plant pots – probably because I accumulate too much! So in my lavender pots, there are magpie and pheasant feathers, in my potatoes purple oyster shells from an estuary and all manner of shells, fossils, and pebbles in other pots. So each pot to me is a small sacred space where a gift of nature is growing and a little gift beside it is a thank you! If you have an altar or sacred space, it only takes a few minutes to pause there, light a candle and recite something that affirms your path and connects you.

Another way of adding into your day is by reading something inspirational and this can be done on the commute, on your coffee break, or even whilst you are in the checkout. Think of the boring times in your day when you are waiting and set up your phone to have something easily available to you. We will look at apps for your phone in a further chapter but there are several that give you daily quotes to consider. Try apps like:

- Thinkup: Positive Affirmations
- Forest: Stay Focused
- Motivation: Daily Quotes
- Daily Quote: Positive Quotes

Some of these inspirational apps also have meditations – and yes you can do them for as little as five minutes! I have to be honest here, I used to be terrible at meditation. I once took a course in pranic healing that involved an hour-long session. Whilst everyone else including the instructor had their eyes closed and was miles away, I was sitting there bored and watching people's faces. I did try to visualise the lovely waterfall they were talking about my magical creatures just kept popping out of the water!

I really struggled with meditation until I found a quick and easy rhythm to it. Nowadays I can zone off for as little as a couple of minutes just to centre myself. My trick was to think more visualisation than meditation and to go with my own imagination rather than what was being suggested to me. Now there is nothing wrong with guided meditation and the OBOD's *Tea with a Druid* on Facebook and YouTube has very short ones (approx. 20 mins) that work really well but I needed to do something that spoke to me. I have a place I go to (in my head!) that's a luscious countryside meadow and I go there to sit and find peace. Because I've done it many times now I can automatically 'land' there and spend as little or as long as I want. Practice does work but its better if it comes naturally to you rather than feeling forced. Think of one of your favourite places and the next time you go to meditate use it as the background to your contemplation.

It's worth mentioning here one of Druidry's key concepts and that is of the awen, pronounced 'ah-when' or 'ah-oo-wen'. It is especially spoken three times in its longer form when intoned in druid ritual and ceremony and is a call for connection to the spirit of inspiration. The 'ah' sound opens you to receiving inspiration. The 'oo' sound is drawn out and allows inspiration to swirl around you. The 'wen' sound ends the intonation and completes the process.

You may have noticed the symbol of awen based on a design by the eighteenth-century Druid revivalist, Iolo Morganwg:

It represents the three rays of light coming from three points of light. But as with many concepts in Druidry, people interpret the rays to mean different things. I like to think of it as nature, knowledge and truth whilst others see it as love, wisdom and truth, three divisions of the soul – mind, body and spirit or the three realms – land, sea and sky or even the upper world, middle world and under world.

It can also represent the three grades of druids – bards, ovates and druids – and today's Order of Bards, Ovates and Druids use these grades for their courses (note – other organisations have a different structure for learning more about Druidry but will often still have three levels). The bards were poets, storytellers, singers, and writers and today the bardic grade opens learners up to the natural world and their own creativity. The ovates were diviners, seers and prophets and this grade digs deeper and teaches you to work with the skills of divination, healing, and the mystic arts. And today's modern druid grade teaches you how to combine all the elements of Druidry and be of service. In times past the druid acted as an advisor to kings, as a judge, a teacher, and as a philosopher. You can be one or some of these things. Some druids like the bardic grade so much they stay there, while others want to rush through training and become it all. Formal training through organisations does differ so some even dip in and out of courses with different organisations to gain other perspectives.

You may have noticed like with the awen there is a bit of a thing about threes! Three sounds when intoning awen, three rays of light, three meanings, three grades, the triple goddess. Three is a sacred and powerful number and never more so when written as a triad – a saying or proverb that comes in threes too. These take only moments to read but much more time to contemplate! *The Triads of Ireland* by Kuno Meyer can be purchased in print or read online at https://www.gutenberg.org/files/31672/31672-h/31672-h.htm. In it you will find many triads to consider like:

- Three things which justice demands: judgment, measure, conscience
- Three hands that are best in the world: the hand of a good carpenter, the hand of a skilled woman, the hand of a good smith
- Three preparations of a good man's house: ale, a bath, a large fire

Welsh triads can be found collected in *Triads of Britain* (1807) by Iolo Morgnnwg, translated by William Probert. Morgnnwg collated triads that he found in medieval manuscripts but also added some of his own.

There are also several other books and collections of wisdom sayings, some of which can be found online. Stick one on a post-it near your work area, write one on a card and place it in your sacred space or tap one into the note function on your phone to look at and consider. Some of my favourites are:

- Three things a person is: what he thinks he is, what others think he is, and what he really is

- Three candles that illume every darkness: truth, nature, and knowledge
- Three things of which everyone is capable, and without which nothing can be: strength of body and mind, knowledge, and love of intuitive wisdom
- Three things one should keep always before them: their worldly duty, their conscience, and the Laws of Nature
- Three teachers of human kind: one is event, that is from seeing and hearing; the second is intelligence, and that comes from reflection and meditation; and the third is genius, individual, a gift from the Mighty Ones

Finally, if you can do nothing else at the end of the day, gratitudes are a simple way to give thanks for all that you have and all that you have been shown. As your head hits the pillow at night, just think of five things you are grateful for. If you are tired they can be as simple as your family, your partner, your pets, your garden, your children etc but if you want to think more deeply you can elaborate on them – I am grateful for the bees that are pollinating the lavender in my garden, I am grateful for the old oak tree that gave me shade today, I am grateful for the inspiration the awen gave me today, I am grateful for the blessings the goddess gave me and most of all I am grateful I am following the druid path. What a way to fall asleep!

Chapter 3

Honouring Ancestors and Deities

Your sacred space, as mentioned in Chapter 2, can also be used to honour the ancestors. In Druidry, we honour three types of ancestors – our blood ancestors, the ancestors of tradition, and the ancestors of the land where we live. By honour I do not mean worship – as said before Druidry is not a dogmatic religion – to some, it is not a religion at all. Honouring is a way to give thanks, to recognise those that came before and to acknowledge what they have meant to us.

Our blood ancestors are our family – the generations who have gone before us. Whether you are into genealogy or not, or know much about your family or not, it took a lot for you to be here today. It took couples having children in a line of descent stretching way, way back, further than any family history site will ever be able to tell you.

Adding small things to your sacred space to honour your blood ancestors can be done quickly with just a bit of thought. Is there a picture of your grandmother or grandfather? A piece of jewellery passed down? An old bowl or cup? A watch or clock? Don't worry if you don't have any family heirlooms – think of what represents your ancestors. Some of mine were straw plaiters so a straw dolly honours years of their toil. Others were watermen so a vial of water represents them.

We often honour our blood ancestors in ways we don't realise like repeating their sayings, cooking a passed-down recipe or wearing heirloom jewellery. Other ways you can honour your blood ancestors are by telling their stories, finding out about the surnames in your family tree or what their occupations were and where they lived.

Honouring your blood ancestors might come more easily to you if you know more about your family history. Think of your ancestors whilst doing your noticing. Is there a plant in your garden that was given to you by a relative? Give it your attention and thanks. Do you walk past a house that a family member lived in? Is there a photo on the wall? Pause and reflect on it for five minutes.

What if you don't know about your blood ancestors? (Or don't want to?) You can have something that just represents past family to you like an angel ornament, a mourning ring or something that signifies your childhood. You can also honour a different type of ancestor instead. Druidry does not come with hard and fast rules and everything can be adapted to suit you.

Ancestors of the land or place – this can be the actual land or house you inhabit or on a bigger scale, the country you live in. For instance, I was unable to trace who had lived in my house before me but they did have an orchard so by placing an apple in my sacred space, it honours the people who came before. Looking at census records might give you an idea but believe me, it will take longer than five minutes. I've lost whole days down that rabbit hole! But say you find out they were a domestic servant, place some soap flakes there or they were an agricultural labourer, add a sheaf of wheat – a small nod to the people who lived in the space you now use.

Find out more about the ancestors of the country you live in. Was there an indigenous race? A clan or tribe that is long gone? I'm in no way advocating cultural appropriation and the assuming of another culture's traditions but, especially in countries where there has been conflict and political strife, it is respectful to honour those who once lived on the land. Consider adding something that symbolises them to your sacred space or place some earth in a small pot to honour all who have walked there before.

Honouring ancestors of place can include finding out more about your locality. Again if you set the intention to notice something new about your garden/land/local area whilst doing a five-minute observation, you might pick up on something to find out more about when you have more time. Do you walk or drive past a sacred site, a market place, a church or graveyard? Is there something new you could learn about the people who once walked the same paths as you do?

Ancestors of tradition – the ancient druids or druids of the eighteenth-century revival like Iolo Morganwg, William Price or George Watson MacGregor Reid or more modern-day druids like Ross Nichols, or people that have meaning to you and have influenced your beliefs – can be depicted in your sacred space or a particular saying or phrase from their written work can be included on a slip of paper.

Honouring ancestors of tradition is sometimes more difficult but ask yourself who has inspired you on your spiritual path. It doesn't have to be a druid – in fact, it is very difficult to pinpoint who really was a druid in history. The history of Druidry is a contentious subject and there isn't scope to get into it here. We don't really know what ancient druids did or didn't do as the records are so scarce. So whereas some people align with druids of old, some ignore the ancient history and just concentrate on modern Druidry and the elements of it that speak to them.

It's also very difficult to define someone else as a druid even if you think their beliefs were such. But there are ancestors of our own traditions. Think of the bardic arts – music, art, storytelling, writing – to name a few and consider who has influenced you in your own creative endeavours.

Who has given you pause for thought? From philosophers to political leaders to people who have changed the world and environmental activists – is there someone in that mix whose words have resonated with you? Add a picture, quote or representation of the work they achieved to your sacred space when contemplating ancestors of tradition.

Deity can be a tricky one for many druids and it can take time to understand your own thoughts and beliefs. Some druids are Christian and believe in God. Some druids are monotheistic – they believe in one God or Goddess whoever that may be, others are duotheists believing in a pair of divine beings, most commonly a god and goddess. Polytheistic druids believe in numerous gods and goddesses – there are a lot out there! Other druids consider the divine is present in all things whilst others believe that by its very nature it cannot be known.

A starting point is a good reference book then all you need is five minutes to dip in and read a quick entry to see if that god or goddess speaks to you and whether you would like to find out more. The publishers of this book also produce titles such as *Gods and Goddesses of Ireland: A Guide to Irish Deities* by Morgan Daimler and *Gods and Goddesses of Wales – A practical introduction to Welsh deities and their stories* by Halo Quin. *The Isles of the Many Gods: An A-Z of the Pagan Gods & Goddesses of Ancient Britain* by Sorita d'Este and David Rankine is also a great, quick dip and is often featured on Kindle Unlimited so is a free read too.

Images or ornaments, statues and figurines can be added to your sacred space to honour your deity/deities. You can buy these or make your own. Once you find out more you'll also find out their associations and these can be gathered or used to symbolise them.

Let's look at some Celtic gods and goddesses:

- Arianrhod is a lunar goddess, associated with fertility and rebirth, spinning, weaving and the silver wheel. Place images of the moon or owls and leaves of ivy or silver birch in your sacred space to honour her.

- Blodeuwedd was created from flowers – meadowsweet, broom, and oak. She is a goddess of emotions. She can be represented by owls and flowers.
- Brigit/Brigid, goddess of poetry, healing, the forge and the spring. You can honour her with flowers, candles, bells and straw Brigid crosses.
- Cerridwen, the keeper of the cauldron of knowledge and goddess of inspiration. Her key symbol is the cauldron and the symbol of awen.
- The Cailleach is a crone goddess and goddess of winter. She can be honoured by placing hawthorn, holly leaves or berries, hag stones and pebbles in your sacred space.
- Rhiannon is a goddess of horses, strength and songbirds. Ornaments or pictures of horses, horseshoes or oatmeal can be placed in your sacred space to honour her.
- The Morrigan is a goddess associated with crows, war and death on the battlefield. The Morrigan is also seen as a triple goddess along with Macha and Badb, her sisters. Symbolise her with black feathers, red candles and black or red crystals such as onyx, garnet and obsidian.
- Arawn, ruler of the realm of Annwn, also known as the Otherworld, the god of death, the afterlife and the guardian of lost souls. Associated with hounds and pigs.
- Cernunnos is a horned nature and fertility god, master of the forest and wildlife, who is associated with nature, grain, antlers, bones, oak leaves and pine cones.
- Lugh is a sun god, associated with ravens and thunderstorms and known for his many skills. As a warrior he is often portrayed with his magic spear and shield. His day is Lughnasa, 1st August, and as such he is associated with the first fruits of the harvest. He can be honoured by including grain, fruit and wine in your sacred space.

- Mabon, Child of Light and the son of the Earth Mother Goddess, Modron, is a god of autumn. He is honoured at the Autumn Equinox. The cornucopia, or Horn of Plenty, filled with pears, damsons, sloes, rose hips, elderberries, blackberries, hawthorn berries, and especially apples can be set out to honour him.
- Manannan mac Lir is a sea god and guardian of the otherworld and the afterlife. Symbolise him in your sacred space with shells, driftwood, pebbles and sea glass.

These are just very brief and basic examples but through research and reading the old texts you can find out more about the gods and goddesses, whether they speak to you and how to honour them with offerings and gifts associated with them.

We have looked at how to honour ancestors and deities in your sacred space but, of course, there are other ways to do so and one of the quickest is to include them in your daily devotions and/or gratitudes. It might be said that you should never rush your connection to deity and that you won't experience a meaningful connection in five minutes but if you have no other time, something is better than nothing.

Starting your day with a devotion of your choice at least aligns your thoughts with your deity, however brief the connection. For example:

O Cerridwen, keeper of the cauldron
I honour you this day
May my brow be bright
May inspiration flow
Awen x 3 (ah-oo-wen)

Whatever the beliefs of any one druid with regard to deities, what we all agree on is the spiritual nature of life. Nature is sacred and divine and you don't have to believe in a god or goddess to practice Druidry if that's not your thing.

Chapter 4

The Wheel of the Year

Druids honour the eightfold wheel of the year. Nature, of course, is cyclical moving through spring, summer, autumn and winter and on again, year after year. The wheel of the year turns, as do our lives. On a grander scale, we move through childhood, adulthood, old age and the final years. But every year our lives also change and during them, we can mark the turn of the wheel of nature's seasons.

There are two solstices in summer and winter, two equinoxes in spring and autumn plus four other special cross-quarter days (also known as Celtic fire festivals) within the calendar that mark sacred times. They are:

- Imbolc – 1st February
- Spring Equinox / Alban Eilir – 21st March
- Beltane – 1st May
- Summer Solstice / Alban Hefin – 21st June
- Lughnasadh – 1st August
- Autumnal Equinox / Alban Elfed – 21st September
- Samhain – October 31st – November 2nd
- Winter Solstice / Alban Arthan – 21st December

The Celtic year typically starts and ends with Samhain but here we will look at a calendar year. Let's look at each of the sacred days in a bit more detail:

Imbolc – 1st February
Imbolc is a cross-quarter day, that falls midway between the Winter Solstice and the Spring Equinox. The word imbolc

21

derives from the Old Irish *i mbolg* meaning 'in the belly', a time of pregnant expectation and the stirring of new life. The grass is beginning to grow, the first flowers are budding, and the days are getting longer. It is a time of rebirth, renewal and hope for a new year.

- Imbolc is traditionally the festival of the goddess Brigid and other goddesses of the hearth
- Ideas for Your Sacred Space: bread, milk, butter, crocuses, a Brigid's cross, candles

Spring Equinox / Alban Eilir (The Light of Regeneration) – 21st March

The heralding in of spring. Night and day are of equal length and there is balance. Soon there will be longer and warmer days. Planting begins and seeds are sown.

- Honour Blodeuwedd, the goddess of spring, flowers and emotions
- Ideas for Your Sacred Space: seeds, coloured eggs, feathers, daffodils

Beltane – 1st May

Beltane and traditionally May Day welcomes the beginning of summer. A cross-quarter day. The sexuality and fertility of life are celebrated. Think of the phallic May Pole and the celebrations that saw many a young girl pregnant. Associated with fire. A time for lovers and the coming together of the goddess and her god.

- Associated with the Horned God and the Green Man
- Ideas for Your Sacred Space: flowers, candles, hearts, ribbons in trees, phallic symbols

Summer Solstice / Alban Hefin (The Light of Summer) – 21st June

The longest and lightest day of the year. The sun is at its full height. The time of the most complex Druid ceremony. Although the sun is at full strength, it is also a time to mark the turning point of the year, for now the sun will begin its decline towards darker days.

- Ideas for Your Sacred Space: yellow and orange flowers, sun pictures and ornaments, red, yellow and orange candles, seasonal produce and sunflower seeds

Lughnasa – 1st August

The beginning of harvest time and a cross-quarter day. The seeds that were sown in spring have grown and now is the time for the plants to ripen and be harvested. A time of abundance and fruitfulness.

- Associated with the sun god Lugh
- Ideas for Your Sacred Space: bread, harvest foods, candles, wheat, corn dollies, barley, first fruits

Autumn Equinox / Alban Elfed (The Light of Autumn) – 21st September

The second of the harvest festivals. It signifies the end of the harvest period. A time when day and night are equal.

- Give thanks to the Earth Mother Goddess, Modron and her son Mabon, the Child of Light
- Ideas for Your Sacred Space: harvest foods, acorns, wheat, berries, wine, dried leaves

Samhain – 31st October-2nd November

Samhain is another cross-quarter day, halfway between the autumn equinox and the winter solstice. It's a time for honouring the dead and our ancestors. It is also a time of settling down for winter and clearing away the old, both physically in your gardens and cupboards and mentally to prepare for the cold months ahead.

- Associated with the Morrigan
- Ideas for Your Sacred Space: apples, pumpkins, gourds, candles

Winter Solstice / Alban Arthan (The Light of the Bear) – 21st December

The shortest day of the year. The time of darkness and death but also rebirth.

- Honour the Cailleach, the goddess of winter
- Ideas for Your Sacred Space: pine cones and needles, holly, mistletoe, poinsettia, ivy

So how can we honour these phases of the year if we have very little time, aren't able to attend a grove meeting or celebration or have little energy? To begin with even just acknowledging them is a start. Put the dates on your calendar or into your phone so you are at least aware that those days are special days within the druid calendar. Here are some other ideas:

- Look at the above ideas and put something in your sacred space that signifies the season whether indoors or out.
- Eat a mindful meal with the produce available in that season.
- Consider your garden – what to grow, what to harvest, what you might grow in the future.

- If you don't have a garden, could you plan a year-round window box or planters so there is something for each season?
- Undertake a quick art project celebrating that day.
- Meditate on what the season or sacred day means both to the world and the environment around you and on what it means to you. Is this a time of year you enjoy? What do you like/dislike most about it?
- Watch online ceremonies and rituals.
- Honour the god or goddess associated with that sacred day or season.
- Read about the old traditions associated with that particular day.
- Jot down words to include in a poem that evokes the day.

There are several ways to honour the wheel of the year, the changing of the seasons and the changing times of our lives. Come up with your own ideas, however small, to mark these special times in the year of a druid.

Chapter 5

The Elements

Druid ancestors revered three Elements, those being Land, Sea and Sky and of course, those are key elements in nature. We more commonly know them as earth, air, fire, and water. Earth fits with the land, water fits with the sea and air with the sky. Some might add fire with sky to include the sun. Sometimes people will discuss a fifth element – the spirit – or the element might differ as in Chinese tradition – wood or vegetation – but to not complicate things too much here we will look at the four basic elements and how you can include them in your practice.

Although druids can work with all the elements you might lean towards one more than another. Here are a few attributes associated with each element. What one speaks to you?

Earth - Groundedness, security, foundation, solidity, strength
Positive qualities – reliability, wisdom, practicality, patience, realism, endurance
Negative qualities – boredom, unobtainable goals, controlling, unhealthy attachments, fear of change
Sign – Capricorn, Taurus, Virgo
Stimulate earth energy by spending time with nature, forest bathing, walking, connecting with trees and gardening
Eat earthy foods like root vegetables and hearty meals like stews and soups

Air – The intellect, thoughts, ideas, intelligence, the mind
Positive qualities – focus, clear-headed, inquisitive, problem-solving, vision, positive thinking
Negative qualities – impatience, harshness, absent-

mindedness, confusion, boredom, distraction
Sign – Libra, Aquarius, Gemini
Stimulate air energy by listening to wind chimes, feeling the breeze in your hair, focusing on your own breathe, deep breathing exercises and by collecting feathers
Air is associated with bitter foods like rocket, turmeric, fenugreek, dandelion, coffee, tea and grapefruits

Fire – Positive energy, passion, action, will
Positive qualities – Powerful, driven, energised, courage, purification, motivation, leadership, courage
Negative qualities – Deceit, cunning, impatient, dictatorial, hot-tempered, erratic, chaotic, bossy
Sign – Aries, Leo, Sagittarius
Stimulate fire energy by watching flames whether it's an open fire or candle, soak up the sun, have a sauna or use a steam room, practice candle-gazing and listen to the sounds of a crackling fire
Flavour foods with hot spices like chilli, cayenne or black pepper, ginger or cinnamon

Water – The emotional world, feelings, sensitivity, receptiveness, reflection
Positive qualities – imagination, intuition, inner growth, dreaming and daydreaming, balancing, calming, embracing the truth
Negative qualities – withdrawal, victimhood, depressed, anxious, negative, or overwhelmed
Sign – Cancer, Scorpio, Pisces
Stimulate water energy by taking a long, hot bath, drinking more water, organising a trip to a beach, lake or river and regularly bathing your face in running water
Eat salty foods (in moderation) like seaweed crackers, celery, tamari, miso or anchovies

Consider which of these you most align with. Whilst you are working with an element, you can dedicate your sacred space to it. For instance, if you are honouring earth, place a pot of soil of some living plants in your area, air can be represented by a feather or windchime, fire by a candle or incense and water by a vial of water, some rock salt or collection of shells. You can, of course, represent all the elements. My sacred space includes, amongst other things, plants, feathers, candles, a water goddess figurine, and fossils.

The elements also correspond to the wheel of the year so if you are decorating your sacred space to reflect the seasons consider which element is in correspondence.

Air – The East, the Spring Equinox, youth
Fire – The South, the Summer Solstice, the Sun at its highest, the prime of our lives
Water – The West, the Autumn Equinox, older age
Earth – The North, the Winter Solstice, death/rebirth

Many druid rituals include a call to the four quarters (cardinal points) and the elements. Your own daily practice can include a call to the elements too. One way is just to turn to each direction (standing or if in a chair you can use your hand) and acknowledge them. For instance, very basically:

I call to the east and the element of air
I call to the south and the element of fire
I call to the west and the element of water
I call to the north and the element of earth

Or you can make it more complex and add in your own thoughts like:

I turn to honour the north and the element of earth
For the life it produces, the trees and plants it nourishes,
For the strength it gives me and the world it sustains
May I be aligned with earth this day

And you can always use meditation as a way of connecting to the elements. If you use YouTube, just look up meditation music for the element you want to focus on and you can use it as a backdrop. You'll find relaxing waterfall or river sounds for water, fire crackling noises, windchimes for air and nature sounds for earth. This can also be helpful if you are stuck indoors but want to feel more connected to nature.

When you can go outside, find a space where you won't be disturbed and for the purposes of a five-minute meditation, pick one of the four elements to connect to. Centre yourself by sitting down and taking three breaths connecting yourself with the sky above you in the first breath, the earth below you in the second breath, and the waters around you in the third breath.

If your focus is earth, you can hold a stone, twig or leaf or place your hands directly on the earth. Feel its solidity underneath you.
If your focus is air, lift your face to the sky and feel the breeze on your face. Listen to leaves blowing in the wind.
If your focus is fire, feel the warmth of the sun on your skin and feel the sun's rays warming the earth around you.
If your focus is water, feel the moisture in the grass or raindrops in the air.

Tuning into the elements around you will help you connect to nature and help you to feel a part of the world around you.

Chapter 6

Sun, Moon and Stars

The sun is the most important source of energy for life on Earth. A hot ball of glowing gases, the sun interacts with the Earth to affect the seasons, ocean currents driven by global wind systems, the weather and climate. We really couldn't live without it.

As such it has been revered for millions of years by cultures across the world. The sun is mainly seen as a masculine energy, although there is some crossover. You can honour the sun through the gods and goddesses who include:

- Áine
- Brigid
- Étaín
- Grannus
- Macha
- Olwen
- Sol
- Sulis Minerva

One of the most simple ways to start the day is to greet the sun, whether it's blazing or hidden behind a cloud. Face its position (please don't look at it!) and outstretch your arms, slowly raising them above your head until your palms are together. Move your hands to your chest level, palms still together and then stretch your arms back out and repeat. I do this every morning three times and it's the time when I say my greeting to the world. It can be as simple as hello sun, hello world! Or you can use the time for your daily devotional whether that is a prayer, an affirmation, a call to a god or goddess or an acknowledgement of the elements and the four quarters.

Other ways to honour the sun include observing sunrise and sunset, sunbathing (don't forget the cream!) and having a sundial in your garden.

The moon is closer to the earth than the sun and we can only see it because it reflects the light of the sun. We also only ever see one side of it – 'the near side', the other is the 'far side' or 'dark side'. And the side that we see changes with what's known as the phases of the moon as it orbits Earth. As the sun lights up different parts of it, it looks as if the moon is changing shape. There are eight phases of the moon that repeat every 29.5 days. They are the new moon, waxing crescent, first quarter, waxing gibbous, full moon, waning gibbous, third quarter and waning crescent.

The moon is seen as feminine energy. Moon goddesses include:

- Cerridwen
- Arianrhod
- Rhiannon
- Juna
- Luna

The triple goddess aspect is often depicted by a woman with a crescent moon on either side of her and is associated with the phases of a woman's life: maiden, mother, and crone. Which goddesses are a matter of some debate and personal preference. The original trinity might have been Persephone the maiden, Demeter the mother and Hekate the crone from Greek mythology. Welsh goddesses could be Blodeuwedd the maiden, Arianrhod the mother and Cerridwen the crone and in Ireland the three sisters Morrígan, Badb and Macha.

Unlike the sun that you should never stare at, the moon offers us a real glimpse of another celestial body and one that is so essential to our lives, controlling our ocean's tides. But how often do we just ignore it especially in the winter when we are cosy and warm indoors?

One evening this year I had the binoculars out as dusk was falling to watch for bats. There weren't any so I decided to just look at the moon and was astonished when I could clearly see the craters on the surface. I can't remember ever doing that before and even through my ancient battered binoculars, it was absolutely stunning.

To honour the moon become aware of its phases. You can track these at https://www.timeanddate.com/moon/phases or at www.moongiant.com. You can also download moon trackers for your phone including My Moon Phase, Ephemeris – Sun and Moon Calendar and Phases of the Moon.

It is believed that ancient druids studied the stars and may have used them as a form of divination. Gregory Clouter writing in *The Lost Zodiac of the Druids* posits that the Gundestrup Cauldron is in fact a map of the druidic night sky. You can read an article about it here www.druidjournal.net/2008/12/11/the-druid-zodiac

You can also use stargazing apps to help you identify them, like these:

- Sky Map
- NASA App
- Star Walk 2
- Star Chart
- SkyView Lite
- SkyWiki

The website www.stellarium-web.org can show you what you can spot from your current location and it also has an app for when you are outside.

If astronomy isn't really your thing, all you need to do is just look sometimes! Sitting out in the garden, wrapped in a blanket, looking with the naked eye or a pair of binoculars can help you to feel connected to a wider world and a far, far wider universe.

Chapter 7

Connecting with Trees

It is often said that the word 'Druid' comes from the word for oak, combined with the word 'wid' meaning to know or have knowledge of. So the term druid could mean 'One with knowledge of the oak'. However, regardless of the roots of the word, connecting with nature and especially trees are one of the most important elements in Druidry. One of the key fundamentals of being a druid is working with a sacred grove – a grove can be external and physical or internal and mental. Druids conduct ritual in physical sacred groves and honour the wheel of the year in ceremony there. Mentally we can escape to our imaginary groves and use that visualisation for inspiration and enlightenment.

I am lucky enough to live in the countryside and have a large garden. In the garden is an area that is my grove. It's not a conventional grove – it isn't circular and has a strange mixture of trees in it from ash and hazel to apple and ginkgo biloba. But it is a place I can go to to meditate, have my morning tea and on a sunny day, work. As I write this I am in the shade of an old ash tree whose trunk has split five ways and whose large branches shelter my writing table. It offers me shade, protection and a constant reminder of the beauty and magnificence of nature.

Without trees we could not survive – it's a plain and simple fact. They give us the air we breathe and are essential to our well-being in so many ways. Trees the world over are in danger and we cannot live without them. Planting trees alleviates the effects of climate change but, of course, you may not have the space or the time to plant your own grove. However, endangered trees, trees that are under threat or species that have already died out need our help and you will find many planting projects you can donate a small amount to or when you have more time could volunteer to help out. For example, One Tree Planted (onetreeplanted.org) is a non-profit organisation focused on global reforestation. They plant trees in Africa, Asia, Europe, North America, Latin America, and the Pacific. For just $1 you can plant a tree in countries where reforestation is needed the most.

Some druid organisations also have planting programmes where trees are planted with reverence and care. The Order of Bards, Ovates and Druids has a Sacred Grove Planting Programme and the Druid Network has begun planting trees in the Caledonian Forest, in Scotland in association with Trees for Life. There are also many tree-planting projects to become involved with or support including:

- Reforest Nation – to reforest Ireland & offset your carbon footprint.
- The World Land Trust – contributes to global reforestation efforts, restoring lost forests, repairing damaged ecosystems and mitigating climate changes.
- Ecosystem Restoration Camps aim is to repair the earth and restore degraded ecosystems from the ground up.
- Reforest Britain is a website that lists major woodland regeneration and urban tree planting projects in the UK.

We can help trees locally and globally but for some of us honouring trees has to be more of an inside project. Not everyone can have an external grove they frequent regularly but in five minutes you can bring one to you! Next time you are on your walk, collect at least four twigs or leaves, to place in the four cardinal directions. If you can gather enough to create a circle all the better. I never pick leaves from trees but you will find lots of discarded debris like twigs, nuts and cones to take home in the autumn and recreate a sacred grove indoors. If you can't get out then ask someone to collect them for you – you don't have to tell them what it's for, it can just be a nature project!

Another idea for bringing a grove indoors is to have bonsai trees. Bonsai is the Japanese art of growing miniature trees in pots. The most commonly found is Fig (ficus) and you can buy these cheaply in supermarkets like Aldi or Lidl but you can also find kits online and grow them from seed. Although many bonsai are native Japanese trees, you can also cultivate other broadleaf evergreens like Myrtle, Jasmine and Eucalyptus, deciduous tree species like Maple, Elm, Birch and Oak or Pines and Conifers like Yew, Cedar, Hemlock and Larch. Bonsai trees have the notoriety of being very difficult to grow but bearing in mind they have limited space to grow, with extra care to water and feed your tree regularly, they can be of great benefit to indoor druids.

Another way of working with trees indoors is to have a piece of wood from the tree you want to work with. You can whittle and carve these yourself but if like me you're clumsy with a knife, you can buy pieces online. I have bought several carved necklaces from Adrian Rooke of Druid Grove Crafts, who creates ogham-carved pendants in a reverential and honourable manner. You can wear them or hang them up indoors and hold them during a five-minute meditation. This book is a direct result of my working with hazel – the tree of inspiration and wisdom – who gave me the idea for this book and even the title! If you can't physically be with a tree, this is a wonderful way to work with them and receive their guidance.

You can also use visualisation if you are unable to be with trees. Imagine you are a tree with your feet planted in the earth reaching down, down like roots into the earth, grounding you. Your arms are branches. Feel your fingers as if they were leaves blowing in the breeze. Lift your head towards the sky, feeling your connection to the sun, the wind, and the rain. Imagine how a tree feels in spring as its leaves begin to unfurl or in winter as leaves are shed. Think of the birds sitting on your branches or squirrels collecting nuts at the base of your trunk. Consider a tree's view – all the things trees have seen as they age – all the changes in the land, the humans that come near them, the creatures that use them for shelter and food, and what the seasons do to the environment. Of course, you can also just have something that symbolises a tree – a crystal world tree, a painting or photo, a carving or an ornament of the tree of life.

If you live in Britain or Ireland the main trees Druids work with are Ash, Birch, Blackthorn, Elder, Hawthorn, Hazel, Holly, Oak, Rowan, Willow and Yew, although there are many, many more and it is really up to the individual to work with whatever tree speaks to them. Let's look at some of the lore surrounding them.

Ash
The world tree or tree of life is associated with a connection to deity and the wisdom it brings.
Used for making druid wands and besom brooms.
Sleep with the leaves under your pillow for prophetic dreams.

Birch
Great for those wanting a new start and a fresh beginning, helps with change.
Used for making maypoles and lighting Beltane fires.
Sweep out the old year with a Birch broom the day after the Winter Solstice or at New Year.

Blackthorn
The greatest protector when going through change and life's upheavals.
Its berries are used for making sloe gin and its wood to make

Irish shillelaghs, walking and fighting sticks.

Be warned though – the blackthorn has sharp spikes and cuts from these thorns can turn septic.

Elder

The Fairy tree that connects us to the Otherworld and helps us to make firm decisions and transition from one stage of our lives to another.

Used medicinally the flowers make an excellent cordial and the berries are rich in vitamin C helping to fight throat infections and respiratory illnesses.

The twigs were traditionally gathered as strong protection against dark magic.

Hawthorn

The tree of lovers helps to heal heartache and strengthen the heart to love again.

Traditionally hawthorn berries are used to make jam, wine and chutney.

In Ancient Greece, brides wore hawthorn crowns.

Hazel

Inspiration and ideas flow when working with this tree that channels awen.

Used for the wattle or wattle and daub building, walking sticks, fencing and baskets.

Hazel or cobnuts are nutrient-rich but are also thought to pass on the wisdom of the tree.

Holly

Protection for the traveller or those fighting for justice

Used for making furniture and traditional Christmas decorations.

One tradition says that if you bring the leaves in in winter, it gives fairies a place to shelter from the cold who will return your kindness by blessing your home.

Oak

The Wise Old Man of trees, ever enduring, full of strength and wisdom.

Used for furniture, flooring and shipbuilding because of its durability.

The most sacred Druid tree, linked to deity through the wrath of the gods and lightning strikes but will continue to thrive even after being struck.

Rowan

Another tree associated with fairies that protects from enchantment and evil powers.

Traditionally used for cart wheels and in boat building.

Sprigs of rowan used to be worn or carried as a protection against evil.

Willow

A healing tree that helps with overwrought emotions and the soothing of wounds.

Used for weaving and has given us salicylic acid used to make aspirin.

The weeping willow became associated with mourning and was used in China for tomb sweeping.

Yew

The tree of death that connects us with our ancestors.

Used for archery bows and musical instruments, however, every part of the tree is poisonous.

Yews were traditionally planted in graveyards, some believe

because of their toxicity so keeping cattle away, others that it represented the body and blood of Christ with its white sap and red berries but even further back it was always associated with death and the journey of the soul from this life to the next.

These are just some of the sacred trees and the lore that surrounds them. The subject is wide and vast and you can find many books on the subject. They may or may not be trees that are local to you. Of course, wherever you are in the world, you will have your own indigenous trees to honour and connect with and some may surprise you.

Trees species, like many animal species, have died out but it is still possible to replant some endangered or extinct species. For instance, in Ireland, a giant redwood forest is being planted at the Giant's Grove in Birr, Co. Offaly. Giant redwoods were once native to Ireland but died out before the Ice Age began about three million years ago. Are there trees that used to grow in your country or your area? Is there an endangered tree you particularly feel connected with and could plant in your garden?

Druids can also use the ogham or tree alphabet that was used for early inscriptions. It is found on stones throughout Ireland and western Britain. Let's see what that looks like:

There are 20 original characters with five fordeda or supplementary characters and they all represent a tree. Below are the first 20 with their tree and corresponding attributions.

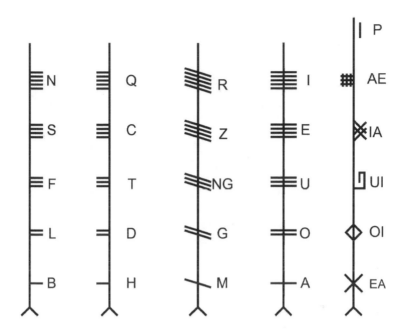

(Runologe, Wikimedia Commons, CC4.0)

B   **Beith** – Birch – New Beginnings, Rebirth, Regrowth, Protection

L   **Luis** – Rowan – Judgment, Protection, Otherworld

F   **Fearn** – Alder – Otherworld, Spiritual Warrior, Strength

S   **Saille** – Willow – Healing, Emotions, Clear Vision

N   **Nuin** – Ash – Interconnection, Justice, Wisdom

H   **Huath** – Hawthorn – Protection in Matters of the Heart

D   **Duir** – Oak – Power, Strength, Wisdom

T   **Tinne** – Holly – Courage, Challenge, Justice

C   **Coll** – Hazel – Inspiration, Awen, Creativity, Messages From The Ancestors, Wisdom

Q   **Quert** – Apple – Celebration, Love, Health, Contentment

M   **Muin** – Vine or blackberry – Freedom, Honesty, Prophecy

G   **Gort** – Ivy – Determination, Dreams into Reality, Joy

NG   **Ngétal** – Reed, broom or fern – Transformation, Healing, Harmony & Light

Z   **Straif** – Blackthorn – Upheaval, Unavoidable Change, Protection

R   **Ruis** – Elder – Endings, Decisions, Transition to Permanent Change

A   **Ailm** – Fir – Vision, Understanding, Clarity, Focus

O   **Onn** – Gorse – Courage, Potential, Abundance

U   **Ur** – Heather – Positive Energy, Harmony, Relationships, Home

E   **Eadha** – Aspen – Endurance, Resistance, Courage

I   **Idho** – Yew – Legacy, Ancestors, Death

We will look at how to use the ogham alphabet for divination or in creative projects in later chapters but for now familiarise yourself with the tree lore for trees in your garden, your local area or ones you travel past every day. What tree calls to you the most? What tree's attributes do you need to tap into at the moment? There are no hard and fast answers. I work with different trees at different times of the year and at different times of my life for different reasons. Druidry is all about what works for you.

Finally, no discussion of connecting with trees would be complete without mentioning the Tree of Life or World Tree also known in Norse lore as Yggdrasil and in Irish lore as Crann Bethadh or Bilé (Bee-leh), the sacred tree. Folklore around the world speaks of sacred trees but the World Tree in Druidry is the one that joins the realms from the Underworld under its roots, to the Middleworld the realm of humans, to the Upperworld the realm of gods and goddesses. It would take far more than five minutes to explain this concept but for now, have a look at some really short YouTube clips to get you in the mood for contemplating the Tree of Life:

- 5 Minute Grounding Meditation, Connect With Earth and Nature Energy For Health and Balance by Sarah Catori https://www.youtube.com/watch?v=Zs8T9xJX55M
- Fantasy Meditation Series Vol. 1: Enchanted Forest | Tree of Life Ambient by Mindful Music https://www.youtube.com/watch?v=pB-mrQ7voEs (this company also has some wonderful short five minute meditations with different nature backgrounds)
- A Minute of Mindfulness - Tree of Life by The Pip https://www.youtube.com/watch?v=L-K31MtEwi0
- 5 Minute Meditation Timer - Tree of Life by Elevation Meditation https://www.youtube.com/watch?v=AFTdt41u2Ww

Chapter 8

Divination

Divination according to two different dictionaries is a) the practice of seeking knowledge of the future or the unknown by supernatural means or b) the art or practice that seeks to foresee or foretell future events or discover hidden knowledge. There are many forms of divination from scrying to using a pendulum or reading tea leaves but the main three in Druidry are tarot, runes and ogham.

In druidic training, finding out more about divination usually comes in the second or ovate level but many of us regularly use divination tools or have dabbled with them in some form. There are, of course, many different ways to divine, from cloud-gazing and scrying to pendulum spinning and dowsing. For the purposes of being a five-minute druid, we will look at extremely easy divination and the methods more commonly used. When you have more than five minutes you can look at more time-consuming ways to use what is discussed below. For now, let's look at some quick and easy ways to incorporate divination into your daily practice.

Tarot or Oracle Cards

Tarot and oracle cards come in many different designs. Tarot decks typically are made up of 78 cards, 22 major arcana and 14 minor arcana cards for each suit of wands, cups, swords and pentacles. But every deck is different and can have variations. For instance, wands can be clubs or staffs, cups could be chalices, swords can be blades and pentacles might be depicted as coins. Generally, the minor arcana usually have page, knight, queen and king cards too.

The major arcana also vary from deck to deck but one version is:

0	The Fool
I	The Magician
II	The High Priestess
III	The Empress
IV	The Emperor
V	The Hierophant
VI	The Lovers
VII	The Chariot
VIII	Justice
IX	The Hermit
X	The Wheel of Fortune
XI	Strength
XII	The Hanged Man
XIII	Death
XIV	Temperance
XV	The Devil
XVI	The Tower
XVII	The Star
XVIII	The Moon
XIX	The Sun
XX	Judgement
XXI	The World

My favourite decks are the Druid Animal Oracle Deck by Philip and Stephanie Carr-Gomm and the Chrysalis Tarot Deck by Toney Brooks. Many moons ago I was also gifted the Cat People Deck by Karen Kuykendall which is old and battered now but remains a treasured possession.

As you can imagine the Druid Animal Oracle contains depictions of revered animals from foxes to dragons and its sister deck the Druid Plant Oracle contains flowers and plants of the Druid tradition. You can also get a combined deck of both as a phone app.

The Chrysalis Tarot deck is based on Otherworld archetypes and a troupe of medieval troubadours. The major arcana includes characters like Merlin, Gaia and the Green Man whilst the minor arcana are split into suits of stones, mirrors, spirals and scrolls.

There are just so many decks out there that if you'd like to use this form of divination you'll really need to do some browsing to pick a deck that suits you and feels right to use. Spreads are as varied as the designs themselves but for the purposes of quick divination, there are three easy readings you could use.

Guidance for the day ahead
In the morning shuffle your cards and with the thought in your mind to seek guidance for the day ahead, pick one card to reveal its message.

*Note if you are new to tarot you might want to purchase a reference guide or book that accompanies your chosen deck for greater insight into your chosen card. As you use them more regularly you will come to remember what the cards mean and not have to consult a book every time you do a reading.

The one card reading
Before you consult the cards, have an idea of what guidance you seek. Think about what issue or problem you need help with as you shuffle them. Select a card you are drawn to and see if its message can help with your situation.

The three-card spread
As above but you choose three cards from the deck. Depending on your intention (what you want the cards to give you focus and clarity on), these can represent different things like past-

present-future, situation-obstacle-outcome or mind-body-spirit for example.

Of course, if you have more time you can develop your use of the tarot and the spreads you use. There is a great website Emerald Lotus Divination that has an online reference library of tarot spreads at https://www.emeraldlotusdivination.com/tarotspreadcollection for you to choose from.

In my own practice, I pick a card of guidance for the day ahead every morning and only use bigger spreads when I need help with a personal issue. Tarot cards will not tell you when you will meet the love of your life, or whether you will inherit a fortune and no, the death card really doesn't mean death! But they can give you insight and aid your self-development. For instance, this morning I drew the Princess of Pentacles which asked me to think about my creative projects in the past and to consider what they will be in the future.

Ogham

Aside from tarot, there are many other forms of divination and one of the most popular is using the ogham. Look back at Chapter 7 – Connecting with Trees – and the image of the ogham alphabet. In Chapter 10 we will see how you can create your own set but for now, you can practice either by using a purchased set, drawing the letters on paper or even by downloading an app for your phone. The ogham symbols are usually carved, burnt or drawn on staves (sticks) and kept in a bag with room to shake and mix them up akin to shuffling tarot cards.

The simplest method of divination is to pick your stave of the day. Shuffle your bag and select one stave. Look up its meaning – its corresponding tree – and its attributions to see whether there is a message for you in its interpretation.

You can also use the stave for a quick past, present and future reading. Shuffle the ogham. Take one stave and place it to the left to represent your past. Take another and place this to your right to represent your future. Lastly, take one more stave and place it in the middle.

For example, say you pick Straif – Blackthorn, Saille – Willow and Beith – Birch. Straif in the past position points to upheaval and change. Saille in the present indicates emotions that need healing and old wounds dealt with. Beith in the future position shows that through your past and present you will reach a point of new beginnings, rebirth and regrowth.

Runes

Whereas the ogham was an Irish early language, runes are native to the Germanic peoples. There are several different runic alphabets including the Elder Futhark (2nd to 8th centuries), Anglo-Saxon runes (5th to 11th centuries), Younger Futhark (9th to 11th centuries) and Medieval runes (12th to 15th centuries). The Elder Futhark, for example, contains 24 runes whilst the Anglo-Saxon has 33.

Casting the runes

Typically inscribed on pebbles or painted on stones, they can also be wooden, crystal, metal or bone and like the ogham kept in a small bag or pouch. Readings too are similar to the ogham but their meanings are far more traditional. For example, the first six runes of the Elder Futhark are:

F	Fehu, meaning domestic cattle or wealth
U	Uruz, meaning a wild ox
T	Thurisaz, meaning a thorn or a giant
H	Hagalaz, meaning hail
A	Ansuz, meaning an ancestral god
R	Raidho, meaning wagon or chariot
K	Kenaz, meaning a beacon or torch

As such they are a bit more tricky to decipher and more modern meanings are been ascribed to them like:

F   Fehu, meaning gain or fulfilment
U   Uruz, meaning strength and determination
T   Thurisaz, meaning brute force or unexpected change
H   Hagalaz, meaning disruption and delays
A   Ansuz, meaning wisdom or knowledge
R   Raidho, meaning travel or journeys
K   Kenaz, meaning positive energy or power

I prefer the Anglo-Saxon runes as displayed in the following chart:

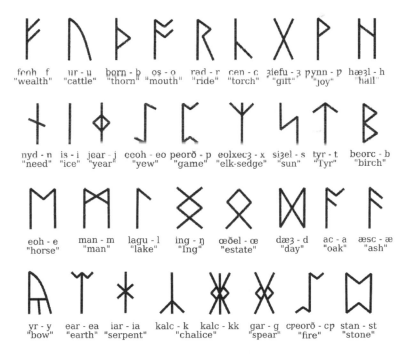

It really is a personal preference as to what runes you would like to use. If you'd like to explore divination with a runic alphabet, look at all the various types and pick the one you would most like to work with.

They can be used like the ogham for picking your rune of the day. A three-rune cast. can also be done quickly to give you insight. As before, consider your query or intention before drawing. Place the selected runes on a cloth in front of you. The first to represent the situation, the second the challenges you will face and the third to represent a possible outcome or the course of action you could take.

In Chapter 9 we will look at creating your own set of runes or, of course, you could purchase a set. Many alternative shops have them available but there are some lovely handcrafted sets on Etsy.

Womanrunes

These are a fantastic deck of cards that are very simple to use and understand. Shekhinah Mountainwater, a key figure in the Goddess movement, experienced what she described as a goddess-lightning strike of inspiration that saw her creating a set of 41 woman-identified rune symbols for divination and personal growth. She described herself as a 'muse-ical mystical magical woman who loves the Goddess and women, a foremother of the Womanspirit movement, a teacher of Women's Mysteries, and a priestess of Aphrodite'. Later author, Molly Remer, expanded on Shekhinah Mountainwater's interpretation of the symbols creating a card deck of the runes and writing a book *Womanrunes: A guide to their use and interpretation* to go with them.

Rather than complicated spreads or readings needing interpreting, the use of womanrunes can be as simple as picking just one card a day. (You can do a short online course at https:// brigidsgrove.com/womanrunes/ when you have the time to find out more). The symbols are basic and simple to copy as a reminder of your draw. For instance, say you chose the circle that's exactly what it looks like – a black line drawn circle meaning rune of the self, beginnings, potential and innocence. Those keywords can then be something to think about during our day.

Just a note to say that there are several different ways of caring for your divination tools from washing to blessing to cleansing. Look up the best way to treat your tools and find a way you are most comfortable with.

Dreams

A lot has been said about dream interpretation and there are thousands of books that will tell you what things in your dreams are supposed to mean. Dream journals can be used to jot down on waking what you saw, felt, heard and experienced in your dream. But dream interpretation is not an exact science and what one book says can vastly differ from the next.

Most of our dreams are just our subconscious sorting through the day's experiences. Ever watched a horror film before you go to bed and then wake up with nightmares? It's just your brain processing and making sense of what you've seen. But your dreams can also be so much more.

Dreams also help us solve problems and sometimes they do it in very creative ways. For instance, I went to sleep thinking about what easy garden projects I could do and as I woke I had the images of several ideas flit through my mind as if my brain had spent the night sorting what was stored to present me with a solution. Sometimes we don't entirely take in what we see, read or hear. We are bombarded every day with so much that we cannot process it all but at night when our subconscious takes over it can sort through all the things we have unconsciously taken in. One study by Bruce Lipton, a Stanford biologist, found that the conscious mind processes information at around 40 bits per second. The subconscious processes more like 20 million bits of information a second. So when we sleep it has free rein and we can use that to help tap into the awen and our creativity by just considering a project before we go to sleep. Don't stay up all night thinking about it. Just suggest it to your mind. Thomas Edison once said 'Never go to sleep without a request to your subconscious.' So set your mind a task before you go to bed. Then on waking take five minutes to jot down any of the ideas that come to you – you might be surprised at how well your subconscious sorts things out if you pay attention to it!

As a druid dreams can also be looked at in a different way especially if you've been working with trees, deities, or ancestors. Did an animal speak to you? Did one of your ancestors appear? Are there messages for you that are coming through in your dreams? These are the things to note in your dream journal and consider when connection is difficult. You might just be receiving messages in your dreams that you have been ignoring.

In Chapter 11 we will look at ways in which you can use social media apps for even quicker divination.

Chapter 9

Reading and Listening

We would all like the time to spend a day with a good book perhaps out on a sun lounger with a cool drink and nibbles or wrapped up in a favourite armchair in front of a roaring fire but quite often this only occurs when we are on holiday or suffering from a cold. Life will always get in the way of a day with a good book and from us feeling we ought to be doing something better with our time.

But snatching five minutes to read something poignant and meaningful can help you connect to Druidry and give you something to consider. Something to ponder as you go about your daily routine.

What can you read quickly? I've mentioned reference books and of course, these are wide and varied. There are a few suggestions at the end of this book but basically, you can go from nature guides to gods and goddesses reference guides to encyclopaedias of mythical beasts to books on Druidry. Books you can easily dip in and out of. Druids amass many books to adorn their bookshelves because there are so many elements included in nature spirituality. If you don't have time to read a heavy tome, find something easier to manage. My husband hates reading but he is a dab hand with a nature book. For beginner druids that can get out and about have a look at Collins pocket gems series, DK's pocket nature or Bloomsbury pocket guides to stick in your bag and carry around with you. They can help you to spot and identify the trees and plants that you come across.

Poetry is easy and quick to read too as are magazine or web articles. Subscribing to a pagan magazine will give you a variety of topics to peruse and leads to follow-up when you have more time. They can also point you in the right direction for events, grove meetings and supplies. Try out these:

- Pagan Ireland
- Pagan Dawn
- Green Egg
- Witches & Pagans
- Crone: Women Coming of Age
- Sacred Hoop
- FAE (Faeries and Enchantment)
- Witchcraft and Wicca
- Touchstone (OBOD members)

There are also some great blogs out there on the world wide web and the articles posted are meant to be absorbed quickly. Have a look at:

- British Druid Order blog https://britishdruidorder. wordpress.com/
- Philip Carr-Gomm's blog https://philipcarr-gomm.com/
- Damh the Bard's blog https://www.paganmusic.co.uk/ blog/
- Down the Forest Path https://downtheforestpath.com/
- Druid Life https://druidlife.wordpress.com/
- The Druid's Garden https://druidgarden.wordpress.com/
- Under the Ancient Oaks https://www.patheos.com/blogs/ johnbeckett/

Triads, quotes, proverbs and sayings are all easy to read in just seconds but can open your mind up and give you something to think about during your day. Sometimes it helps to read them aloud too and roll the words around your tongue, speaking them more than once. Find one you like and keep repeating it to yourself and you will find you will soon remember it.

You can also get books of quotes that are easy to dip into. Try *By Time Is Everything Revealed: Irish Proverbs for Mindful Living* by Fiann O'Nuallain, *The Proverbs of Wales: A Collection of Welsh Proverbs, With English Translations* by T R. Roberts or a more general book like the *Little Oxford Dictionary of Proverbs* by Elizabeth Knowles.

Podcasts are a great way to listen to interesting information and you can listen for as long or as short as you like. You can tune in on your computer but the best way is to download a listening app suitable for your phone like Spotify, Google Play Music, Apple Podcasts or Castro. You can stop and start them, rewind or pause so you can always go back and listen to that little bit more. There are shows that specifically discuss Druidry including:

- Druidcast
- Druid Wisdom
- Three Witches and a Druid
- Druids in Cars, Going to Festivals
- Forest Spirituality with Julie Brett

And then there are others on topics like folklore, myths and legend, nature, ecology, paganism and deity like:

- The Folklore Podcast
- Tales of Britain and Ireland
- The Loremen
- Nature Podcast
- Nature Tripping
- Backyard Ecology
- Ecology Matters
- Down at the Crossroads
- Three Pagans and a Cat
- Once upon a Goddess

- Irish Mythology Podcast
- Celtic Myth Podshow

There really is something for everyone and something different for you depending on your mood, interest and how much time you've got. Some podcasts have short five-minute episodes, whilst others are an hour long but you can always dip in and out of them when you have a spare five minutes.

If you don't have time to read, you might have more time to listen! Many books are available now as audiobooks. Amazon has its Audible programme but there are others like Scribd, Overdrive, and Libby that will let you listen via your phone or computer.

Songs don't usually take that long to listen to either! Have you thought of listening to stories put into song or spoken word music? Damh the Bard (www.paganmusic.co.uk) has produced some fabulous music but especially those that tell the tales of the Mabinogion – three branches so far – entitled Y Mabinogi.

Other tale weavers who put words to music include Dani Larkin, Seth Lakeman and the Bog Bodies. Musicians such as Spiral Dance, S J Tucker, Cernunnos Rising, and Gaia Consort combine folklore and myth with music and their songs can take you to another place!

Chapter 10

Writing and Drawing

Finding the time to write anything of length can be a trial – I know, I've written several books! Saying that, if writing a book has always been your goal and you'd like to write about an aspect of Druidry, you could start to plan your book in as little as five minutes a day! Use short periods of time to decide what chapters you would include in your book and when you have those set what each chapter will cover. There's a great cognitive behavioural therapy tool called 'breaking down' that you can use for almost any task. Think of the main goal like writing a book but then break it down into small, manageable bite-sized achievable actions like listing how many chapters – say 10 – and each day in your allotted five minutes come up with a chapter title. It may not be much but it is a start!

You can also do this for articles. Think of an article you want to write and jot down the key points you want to cover. Check back to the list of Pagan magazines in the previous chapter – many of them take submissions from articles to poetry to drawings.

Keeping a daily journal doesn't need to take more than a couple of minutes a day. Not everyone likes keeping a diary but as we saw in the chapter on divination you can use them to keep a track of the experiences, ideas and meetings you have in dreams and they can also be used to jot down your findings when you have been noticing and observing so when you have more time you can look back and pick something to delve into more deeply.

Poems can be created in five minutes! It may not be a masterpiece but then how do you know unless you try! First close your eyes, still your mind and open up your senses. Write down the first thought you have. It could be something you can hear – like at the moment I can hear the rain outside so ok – *Rain is falling on the roof* – that's a first line. Then think about how that sound makes you feel. After weeks of sunny weather to me it is – *A blessing for the parched earth* – line two! Then think of a final line, a result or resolution – it's going to nourish and help everything to grow again so *Turning brown once more to green*. There we have it – not the world's most subtle poem but a poem nonetheless:

Rain is falling on the roof
A blessing for the parched earth
Turning brown once more to green

If you love poetry as I do, just practice putting thoughts and feelings together and see what you come up with! You can always send it to a magazine to see if they like it too.

We looked at triads – wisdom sayings that come in threes in Chapter 2 but how about making up your own? Just remember they come in threes. Try something really simple to start with like the best thing about dogs: loyalty, companionship, protection or the best things about trees: shelter, wood, leaves – just to get you into the flow of thinking in threes. Then expand it to wider concepts like the three secrets of a good marriage or the three secrets of a long life – you can go as deep as you want!

If you are completely stuck and don't even feel like writing anything of depth just jot down words. Create a mind map of ideas and thoughts. Start with a key concept like Druidry for instance and draw lines coming off of it. List other words (or you can use drawings) and see where that branch sends you. Say you write down Druidry – trees – where might that lead you? Leaves, branches, roots – the physical attributes and then perhaps what they mean to you – shelter, protection, air – and each of these words can send you off again.

Mind maps are a visual representation of your thoughts and ideas and you can use them to help you work out where you going on your path and what you would like to concentrate on. Try starting with the concept – me as a druid – and see where it takes you. You might find you jot down the main elements like ancestors, elements, trees, wheel of the year etc but see what branch you end up following. You might find you ignore or get stuck on some of them but others will flow and subconsciously you will mind map the areas you are most interested in.

In Chapter 8 on divination, we looked at runes letters, the ogham and womanrunes. You can practice learning the symbols and their meanings by drawing them on card or paper. If a particular rune speaks to you, draw it and place it in your sacred space so you can see it regularly. You can also practise writing sentences with runes. Start by just spelling your name. For instance, in Anglo-Saxon runes, my name Sarah looks like this:

ᚻᚠᚱᚠᚻ

If you have someone to practice with you could send them little notes to decipher like:

ᛁ ᛁᚠᚠᛗ ᛁᚠᚢ
ᚦᛗ ᛚᚠᛏ ᚾᛗᛗᛞᛋ ᚠᛗᛗᛞᛁᚷ
ᛞᛁᚾᛏᛗᚱ ᛁᛋ ᛁᚾ ᚦᛗ ᚠᚠᛗᚾ

Translation: I love you, the cat needs feeding, dinner is in the oven!

You can have great fun with rune sentences and given get the kids to draw them. You can find a rune translator at https://valhyr.com/pages/rune-converter or at https://www.vikingrune.com/rune-converter/ where there is a choice of Elder Futhark,

Anglo-Saxon runes, Long Branch Younger Futhark, Short Twig Younger Futhark and staveless runes.

Have a look back at the womanrunes section in Chapter 8 – they are so simple yet powerful symbols. On their website (https://brigidsgrove.com/womanrunes/) they state that they are 'very easy to use directly yourself—including them in your own art, drawing or etching them onto objects, and thereby writing them into your consciousness in a living manner'. Choose a symbol that speaks to you and draw it on a card to prop in your sacred space or to carry with you. You can make it as plain or as pretty as you like.

But you could also consider developing your own runes using symbols that speak to you. Plain postcard-size card can be purchased in craft shops and you could use five minutes a day to just think of a word and a symbol that represents it. Think of things you would ask the runes about – it could be love, strength, health, or wisdom for example. Then consider a simple symbol that would depict this – love is typically a heart but it could be an infinity symbol or lips, strength could be a bear's pawprint or a lotus flower, health could be a red cross or the eye of Horus and wisdom an owl or a book. The possibilities are endless and you can go from very simple symbolic designs to more complicated drawings when you have more time.

If you are so inclined you could also start working on your own tarot deck. It will obviously take some planning but you can buy blank playing cards to practice on. And when you have a spare five minutes, consider what concept or theme you would like to use. For instance, do you like fantastical beasts? Or what about trees? Maybe crystals and stones? Then once you have decided that, you could start envisioning what each card would look like. You can gradually build your deck with your own depictions. Once you have a deck together, you can have them printed as cards. There are many online cheap printers that offer the service and they can even be given as gifts to friends!

Some druids also like to use sigils in their practice. Sigils are magical symbols that can be imbued with intention. Think of the awen with its three dots and three rays or the tree of life. There is also a druid symbol of a round circle with two lines which is sometimes depicted as a wreath of leaves with two branches across it. Or what about the Celtic symbols like the triskele or triquetra (threes again!)? Some are extremely simple in design, others more complicated. Sigils are easy to draw with any medium; pencils, markers, chalks, paint etc and can be drawn on everything from card to wood to ceramics. They can be used to meditate with or placed in your sacred space to contemplate.

Of course, just sitting with paper and pencils or paper and paint is one of the easiest and quickest ways to get creative but consider doing it with intent. Think of an aspect of Druidry that you love – the sun, the elements, trees, a deity – and then give yourself free rein to just sketch, doodle or paint the things that call to you.

Mandalas are seen as a way to connect your inner worlds and outer worlds by an expression of pattern and shape in a circular design. The word 'mandala' means circle in Sanskrit but its use is akin to meditation as you gradually build the layers of your pattern. The first mandalas were thought to be created by Buddhist monks during the first century BC and are often based on patterns found in nature. Basically, there is a picture in the middle of the mandala often a flower or leaf motif and then around it five or six circles of varying patterns. Some artists use a compass to mark out the wheels of a mandala but you could find something in your home to draw around like different sizes of bottles or jars. You can also go completely freehand – hey it might not end up a perfect circle – but who cares? Have a look at some mandala pattern designs (just search for simple mandala images in your browser – there are hundreds!) and create your own version.

If you've collected natural materials like twigs, pine cones and leaves that you are about to chuck out why not dip them in paint first and make a picture using nature itself? Got old flowers in a vase? Coat the petals with different colour paint and make prints with them. Autumn leaves in the drive? Collect a handful and make leaf prints. Look at what is around you and use it to inspire your creativity and unleash your creative side.

Chapter 11

Social Media and Apps

Social media is a two-headed beast – one consumes voraciously, and the other watches and learns. Whether you use social media or not, it's now a factor in everyday life and is never going away. For those of us who use it regularly, it can be a way to connect with family, work and our interests but it can also suck quality time out of our day.

When we talk of using five minutes to support our Druidry we should stop and consider how long we use social media for and whether it is reinforcing our beliefs or whether we spend more time looking at funny animals, depressing news or the latest celebrity crisis. Are we voraciously consuming meaningless matter? Yes, social media can be used to unwind and relax but really how much of it is truly relaxing? For every couple of posts that are meaningful, there are twenty more that make us feel uncomfortable.

We can focus our use of social media, however, to support our path by following druid organisations, ecology initiatives, nature sites, inspirational people and support groups of like-minded people. We can watch and learn rather than focusing on trivial matters.

All the major druid organisations have social media feeds whether it be on Facebook, Twitter or Instagram including:

- Order of Bards, Ovates and Druids
- British Druid Order
- AODA – Ancient Order of Druids in America
- Anglesey Druid Order – Urdd Derwyddon Môn
- Black Mountain Druid Order
- The Green Mountain Druid Order

Have a look to see what national orders there are in your own country and what local groups you could follow. Out of all social media – and you can argue with me! – I find Facebook to be the most engaging. There are groups to follow and be involved in. The Order of Bards, Ovates and Druids for example has several offshoot groups like:

- Order of Bards, Ovates and Druids – Members' group
- OBOD Friends
- Friends of OBOD and Druidry
- Obodies in Ireland
- OBOD Artists Community
- OBOD Divination Discussion – An OBOD Members' Group

Don't want to be affiliated with a particular order? Then have a look at groups such as the Druid Forum, Druid's Worldwide Grove, Druid Circle, Druid or Irish Druids. They can be a great source of support as well as giving you a creative outlet to share your thoughts or projects in.

For instance, on a visit to a national garden recently I saw they had giant dreamcatchers in the trees. My partner and I made one for our garden – that was one project that was way more than five minutes! – but I took a picture of it and shared it with a druid group. Sharing takes just seconds and your creativity might just spark someone else's. It's a way of seeing other people's bardic pursuits and other ways in which their Druidry manifests and in turn, you can receive feedback on your own.

I would also suggest that you do a quick recce of who and what you follow. If like me you've built this up over the years it is going to take time – more than five minutes – but once it's done, you've had a clear-out and you can then follow people and pages that spark something in you.

- Do you love trees? Follow Britain's Ancient and Sacred Trees on Facebook.
- Interested in veganism? Try @rVeganLobby on Twitter.
- Love a funny podcast? Follow shoveitupyourawen on Instagram.
- Want to share your projects? Join the OBOD Artists Community on Facebook.
- What to be more connected to like-minded people? Follow @PagansInTouch on Twitter.
- Want some inspiration? Follow druidsgardenart on Instagram.
- Love your folklore? Have a look at Folklore, Customs, Legends and Mythology on Facebook.
- Want to just dip into something Druidry? Follow @ druidscauldron on Twitter.
- Need more books to read? Follow moonbooksjhp on Instagram.

There are so many groups, people and organisations out there so have a look and pick the ones that speak to you and your current focus. From Celtic deities to ogham divination, there are pages and groups to look at so that when you do use social media it's a better use of your time.

The key is to not spend hours on it. And when you have that spare five minutes you can engage with social media that reminds you of elements of Druidry and could spark an idea for your own practice or your sharing could help someone else's.

There are also message boards, forums or discords if you are a member of a particular organisation. Sending a like, a supportive comment, or posting a quick message can make you feel more connected and can help you to build your sense of being a part of the druid community.

Applications on your phone are a great way of quickly and effortlessly engaging. Most have a notes app pre-installed so that you can just pop a few lines down to remind yourself to look into something at a later time or you can download a specific app like Notepad, Evernote or Simplenote. It could be anything from a song to download, a line of a poem you are working on or a book to purchase. I have a creative ideas list on the go at all times for when I have the opportunity to focus on a project so when I think of something I would like to try like making a clay goddess, a garden sculpture or designs for oracle cards I jot them down. I might never get to the end of the list but hey, the ideas are there!

As I mentioned in the chapter on noticing, there are also handy apps that just take seconds to help you to identify the trees and plants that you come across. Google lens is a free app that searches the internet for a match when you have taken a picture. I find it does have some difficulty in differentiating types of plants and insects relying mainly on US sites but it can be handy while you are on the go and if you have some idea of what you are looking at. Some free identifier apps also to try:

- British Tree Identification by Woodland Trust
- Deciduous Trees 2.0 Lite is a free version of Deciduous Trees and is a tree identification app focusing on conifers
- Identitree Starter Kit is a simple-to-use app that identifies trees by asking you questions about the branches, twigs, and leaves
- PlantNet, iNaturalist and PlantSnap are plant identifiers
- eBird, Merlin Bird ID and Raptor ID are bird identifiers
- Song Sleuth is a birdsong analyser
- Herbs Guide

This is just a brief selection of nature identifiers and you can get apps that will identify anything from mushrooms and bugs to stars and constellations.

More sophisticated versions can be found on Google Play or the Apple store to purchase but I discovered that many of the free apps are fine, it is just a matter of trial and error to find the most suitable one for you that's easy to use. And once it's installed on your phone, will take less than five minutes to help you identify something you find.

Applications are wide and varied but there are a couple more that I have found really useful, quick and easy to use that have helped me along my path. One is a language app that you have probably heard of and that is Duolingo which has over 40 languages to learn. In the past, I have used it to brush up on my French and learn a little Latin but now I'm using it to learn Welsh after studying many of the Welsh stories and legends and wishing I could read them in their original versions.

Other Welsh language learning apps include:

- Learn Welsh. Speak Welsh. Study Welsh.
- Say Something in Welsh

And there are also Welsh-English translators and dictionaries readily available at no cost. These are apps that you can easily dip into for a few short minutes. I find that with Duolingo it encourages you to practice every day so for five minutes after breakfast I do a couple of exercises and then wander around for the rest of the day repeating phrases!

The other type of apps that I have found interesting to use are divination apps and more specifically the tarot. A company called The Fool's Dog have a variety of apps including DruidCraft, Wildwood Tarot and the Druid Oracle Cards. These do cost but I have never paid more than £5 for any of them. There are also free tarot apps from other developers.

And there are many other types of divination apps out there like:

- Oghamantis
- Runic divination
- Lenormand Tarot
- Galaxy Runes

Now I know many people may be thinking you can't properly divine or have an accurate reading from a phone application and there is most definitely something to be said about using the traditional methods but we are talking about a quick, five-minute action to support your druid path. The apps I use have a full range of spreads but they also have 'today's card'. This gives you an image from a popular deck like the Druid Oracle cards and its meaning which can be read in less than five minutes but thought about throughout the day.

Other apps of interest include moon tracking, the wheel of the year, the pagan calendar, crystal identification, meditation and believe it or not there is also one for candles so if you need one for a ritual, you can watch a virtual one!

Chapter 12

Five Minute Creative Projects

In this chapter, we are going to look at quick five-minute creative projects that will engage your bardic and creative skills and open you up to inspiration. Remember that saying that if you ask five druids what Druidry means you will get ten different answers? Well, arts and crafts are like that. Give five druids a creative medium and you will get ten different ideas for creative projects! I watched a glass-blowing competition recently where ten artists were given one theme and ten different pieces were created. The theme was interpreted ten different ways because each artist has their own background, beliefs, likes and dislikes that inform their work. Sometimes all you need is that little spark, that gift of awen, that inspires you to create something unique to you.

Many of us think it is meaningless or childish to play with clay, paint a picture or make puppets but by just trying something new, you tap into awen and you create. It doesn't matter whether it's good or bad – no one is looking unless you want to share – and freeing yourself to new techniques and new experiences can lead to bigger and better things. We suppress as adults what we so easily did as children and we should reclaim our creativity, let go and be in the moment, giving room for inspiration to flow.

When I was stuck in bed after my accident, I ordered many different kits to inspire me to do something in my better moments. Some of those were a bit ambitious like diorama kits, lino cutting and jewellery making but you don't have to spend a lot of money or go for anything very complicated. I've found some really quick, cheap and easy kits in the toy sections of supermarkets from making bug hotels to bird boxes you just click together and paint.

Clay isn't expensive and if you get the air-drying stuff you can break a project down into two stages – making and painting. Of course, you can make complicated projects but you can also make very simple things in five minutes like an offering bowl or incense holder. If you have a sacred space – indoor or outdoor – you could try making little bowls with an easy pattern on them. Let them dry usually for 24-72 hours and then paint. If there are going outside or will be used for liquids, varnish them as well. These can be used to place seeds, grain, or flowers in when honouring a deity.

One to do with the kids is peg dolls or in my local supermarket, they have wooden cut-out figures on sticks. They only take five minutes to decorate with pens, stickers, or stick-on jewels but you could also use cloth and fabric if you had more time. These are great for storytelling props and help to enliven a retelling of a myth or legend.

Pebble runes are so simple to make! Check which runic alphabet you'd like to use, collect pebbles from the beach or stones from a path and using paint pens or markers, draw on the symbols. Hey, presto! Your own rune set for divination is made in five minutes. You can also make your own ogham staves in this way by drawing the tree alphabet onto 25 small sticks. Choose the sticks to all be of a similar length or cut down (you can also use some old dowel cut up into sections). If you have more time you could carve or wood burn the letter of the alphabet onto your sticks but if not a black marker or paint pen will suffice.

Pebbles or smooth round stones can also be painted to leave as kindness gifts. Paint pens are great for these but to make them last, give them a lick of varnish. The Kindness Rocks Project was started by Megan Murphy in 2015 who wrote 'You've got this' on a rock and left it on a beach on Cape Cod. Since then there have been lots of different positivity pebble projects but the main idea is to paint or write an inspirational message on a pebble and leave it somewhere for someone else to find.

Photography has become so simple if you use your phone. Of course, you can have the best of equipment if you like but just taking a photograph of a stunning tree, a beautiful flower or an interesting landscape takes seconds. Your phone will hold them for you to look back on or you can save them to your computer and use them as desktop backgrounds to remind yourself of the wonders you have seen. You can also share your pictures in Facebook druid groups if you think other like-minded people might be interested in seeing them.

Here's another outside activity – nature art! On a recent holiday, I found a coffee table book in our accommodation about art in the wild and the ideas were just so simple. Like the pebbles you leave for someone to find, these are quick and easy to put together on your walk and it leaves behind something for someone else to stumble upon and wonder about. It can be as simple as making a pattern on the path with fallen leaves, building a stick pyramid, carving a pattern in the sand or using pebbles to create a spiral or other pattern. The next time you are out and about see what material is around you and create something that will amaze and amuse people. Ever see messages in the sand when you walk along a beach and wonder who put them there whilst knowing it is not going to last? This is the same thing. You make a temporary art installation for people to come across and it might just brighten someone's day.

To attract more birds to your garden, how about a quick and easy bird feeder? If it's the right time of the year, collect pine cones. Attach string at one end and fill with birdseed. Or the next time you have an orange scoop the flesh out from one half and fill the bowl with seed. Or a mucky but really effective one is to smear old toilet rolls with peanut butter and then roll in birdseed. You can then slot them on a tree branch in the garden.

When you're planting veg or herbs whether outside or in pots, you can use paint pens to write on a wooden spoon or pebble what seed you've sown or decorate some pebbles to add to your garden as a feature by creating a spiral or other pattern. You could decorate a pebble a day or once a week in your spare five minutes and gradually build up a collection for putting outside.

If you can't get outdoors easily how about some crafts to bring the outside in? Paper flowers or origami flowers can be easily made and used to adorn your sacred space. Paint some pine cones in different colours and glue twigs to the bottoms so that they look like flowers. Gathered together in a vase they will brighten up any room. Use cardboard to make a 3D tree and decorate each branch with colourful leaves. Use seeds or dried pulses from the cupboard to create a mosaic nature picture (with card and glue) or create a rune or ogham symbol from these natural materials to add to your sacred space.

Colouring-in might seem like a childish occupation but just look at how popular adult colouring books are these days. It's a completely relaxing activity and you can use whatever medium suits you from pencils and pens to paint and pastels. Look in any bookstore or arts and crafts shops for colouring-in books. I also like colouring cards and am currently working on a set of mandala cards. These can be mounted and used as birthday cards or pinned on the wall to decorate a boring space.

Did you ever as a child doodle random lines and swirls on a piece of paper and then colour them in? There's a more grown-up meditative method called zentangling created by Rick Roberts and Maria Thomas. You basically take a piece of card, put a dot in each corner and join them up for a border. Then you draw a line between two opposite dots – straight or curvy you choose – to divide up your card. In each section, you then doodle a pattern and the patterns can be as simplistic or complicated as you want. Check out www.zenangle.com for more ideas.

Some of these suggestions might seem pointless or childish to you but if you are struggling to connect then sometimes, by just working on a simple and easy craft project, it allows you to just be and in that quiet being you are opening yourself up to a world of future possibilities.

Epilogue

I hope that some of these ideas will inspire you and aid you along your Druidic path. Some days we will have all the time in the world to contemplate our spirituality but other days we will be pushed to even think of it.

But if like me you feel the need to do something to make your connection easier then I hope this book has given you some suggestions. From connecting with trees to creative projects and more, there are many ways to include Druidry in your everyday life.

Some of these can be accomplished quickly but others can be developed over time when you can pay them more attention. There are so many aspects to Druidry that even just dipping into a book like this can give you new pathways to follow and new interests to find out more about.

I wish you well on your journey!

Further Reading

A Book of Pagan Prayer by Ceisiwr Serith

A Brief History of The Druids by Peter Berresford Ellis

A Druid's Herbal by Ellen Evert Hopman

A Druid's Herbal of Sacred Tree Medicine by Ellen Evert Hopman

A Treasury of Irish Myth, Legend, and Folklore by W.B. Yeats and Lady Gregory

A World Full of Gods by John Michael Greer

Ancient Irish Tales, edited by Cross & Slover

Blood and Mistletoe by Ronald Hutton

Celtic Gods, Celtic Goddesses by R.J. Stewart

Celtic Mythology by Prionsias Mac Cana

Celtic Myths and Legends by Peter Berresford Ellis

Celtic Tree Mysteries by Steve Blamires

Dictionary of Celtic Myth and Legend by Miranda J. Green

Druid Magic: The Practice of Celtic Wisdom by Maya Magee Sutton & Nicholas Mann

Druid Mysteries: Ancient Wisdom for the 21st Century by Philip Carr-Gomm

Druidcraft: The Magic Of Wicca & Druidry by Philip Carr-Gomm

Druidry and Meditation by Nimue Brown

Druids, Gods and Heroes from Celtic Mythology by Anne Ross

Druids: A Very Short Introduction by Barry Cunliffe

Early Irish Myths and Sagas translated by Jeffrey Gantz

Exploring the World of the Druids by Miranda Aldhouse-Green

From the Cauldron Born: Exploring the Magic of Welsh Legend & Lore by Kristoffer Hughes

Her Sacred Britannia: The Gods and Rituals of Roman Britain by Miranda Aldhouse Green

How to Charm a Dryad by Penny Billington

Irish Fairy & Folk Tales by W.B. Yeats

Ogham: Weaving Word Wisdom by Erynn Rowan Laurie
Pagan Celtic Britain by Anne Ross
Sacred Fire, Holy Well: A Druid's Grimoire by Ian Corrigan
The Ancient Celts by Barry Cunliffe
The Awen Alone by Joanna van der Hoeven
The Bardic Source Book edited by John Matthews
The Book of Celtic Magic by Kristoffer Hughes
The Book of Druidry by Ross Nichols
The Celtic Seers Source Book: Vision and Magic in the Druid Tradition
     by John Matthews (editor)
The Complete Idiot's Guide to Paganism by Carl McColman
The Druid Magic Handbook: Ritual Magic Rooted in the Living Earth
     by John Michael Greer
The Druid Renaissance by Phillip Carr-Gomm
The Druid Revival Reader by John Michael Greer
The Druid Way by Philip Carr-Gomm
The Druidry Handbook by John Michael Greer
The Druids by Peter Berresford Ellis
The Druids by Ronald Hutton
The Druids by Stuart Piggot
The Encyclopedia of Celtic Wisdom by John and Caitlin Matthews
The Mabinogion translated by Sioned Davies (translation by
     Patrick Ford is also recommended)
*The Mist-Filled Path: Celtic Wisdom for Exiles, Wanderers, and
     Seekers* by Frank MacEowen
The Mysteries of Druidry: Celtic Mysticism, Theory & Practice by
     Brendan Cathbad Myers
The *Pagan Portal* series
*The Pagan Religions of the Ancient British Isles: Their Nature and
     Legacy* by Ronald Hutton
The Path of Druidry: Walking the Ancient Green Way by Penny
     Billington
The Solitary Druid: A Practitioner's Guide by Robert Lee Ellison

The Táin: From the Irish epic Táin Bó Cúailnge translated by Thomas Kinsella

The Tree of Enchantment by Orion Foxwood

The Triumph of the Moon by Ronald Hutton

The World of the Druids by Miranda Green

What Do Druids Believe? By Philip Carr-Gomm

Where the Hawthorn Grows: An American Druid's Reflections by Morgan Daimler

Witches, Druids, and King Arthur by Ronald Hutton

Internet Resources

Orders

Anglesey Druid Order – Urdd Derwyddon Môn: www.angleseydruidorder.co.uk

AODA – Ancient Order of Druids in America: www.aoda.org

Avalon Druid Order: https://www.avalondruidorder.org

Black Mountain Druid Order: www.blackmountaindruidorder.com

British Druid Order: www.druidry.co.uk

Druidry US – A place for United States OBOD members: www.druidryus.org

Irish Druid Network: www.irishdruidnetwork.org

Little Druid on the Prairie: www.prairiedruid.com

Order of Bards, Ovates and Druids: www.druidry.org

The Druid Network: www.druidnetwork.org

The Druid Order: http://thedruidorder.org

The Green Mountain Druid Order: www.greenmountaindruidorder.org

Courses

Order of Bards, Ovates and Druids: www.druidry.org/our-courses/train-in-druidry

The British Druid Order: www.druidry.co.uk/courses

Grove of Anu: www.groveofanu.com/druid-course-introduction-to-the-tradition-of-druidism

Anglesey Druid Order : www.angleseydruidorder.co.uk/courses

AODA: www.aoda.org/aoda-membership/curriculum-requirements

Isle of Wight order of Druids: www.wightorderdruids.com/druid-of-the-birch-grove-course-1

Druid Forest School: https://druidforestschool.com/courses

Other

Triads: https://www.gutenberg.org/files/31672/31672-h/31672-h.htm.

Tarot: https://www.emeraldlotusdivination.com/tarotspreadcollection

Womenrunes: https://brigidsgrove.com/womanrunes/

Rune Converter: https://www.vikingrune.com/rune-converter/

Honouring Deity: https://www.learnreligions.com/appropriate-worship-honoring-the-gods-2561946

The Eightfold Wheel of the Year: https://druidry.org/druid-way/teaching-and-practice/druid-festivals/the-eightfold-wheel-of-the-year

The Morrigan
Meeting the Great Queens
Morgan Daimler
*Ancient and enigmatic, the Morrigan reaches out to us.
On shadowed wings and in raven's call, meet the ancient Irish
goddess of war, battle, prophecy, death, sovereignty, and magic.*
Paperback: 978-1-78279-833-0 ebook: 978-1-78279-834-7

The Awen Alone
Walking the Path of the Solitary Druid
Joanna van der Hoeven
*An introductory guide for the solitary Druid, The Awen Alone will
accompany you as you explore, and seek out your own place
within the natural world.*
Paperback: 978-1-78279-547-6 ebook: 978-1-78279-546-9

Moon Magic
Rachel Patterson
*An introduction to working with the phases of the Moon,
what they are and how to live in harmony with the lunar
year and to utilise all the magical powers it provides.*
Paperback: 978-1-78279-281-9 ebook: 978-1-78279-282-6

Hekate
A Devotional
Vivienne Moss
*Hekate, Queen of Witches and the Shadow-Lands, haunts the pages
of this devotional bringing magic and enchantment into your lives.*
Paperback: 978-1-78535-161-7 ebook: 978-1-78535-162-4

Readers of ebooks can buy or view any of these bestsellers by clicking on the live link in the title. Most titles are published in paperback and as an ebook. Paperbacks are available in traditional bookshops. Both print and ebook formats are available online.

Find more titles and sign up to our readers' newsletter: johnhuntpublishing.com/paganism

For video content, author interviews and more, please subscribe to our YouTube channel.

MoonBooksPublishing

Follow us on social media for book news, promotions and more:

Facebook: Moon Books Publishing

Instagram: @moonbooksjhp

Twitter: @MoonBooksJHP

Tik Tok: @moonbooksjhp